Dream Dictionary

A Convenient Dictionary of Dream Symbols for Interpreting Dreams Accurately

by Dhara Pierce

Table of Contents

Introduction

Dreams have always held humanity's fascination, and for the longest time, people have been yearning to uncover the meaning of their dreams.

What do our dreams mean? Are dreams separate from our reality or do they have a connection with our conscious state? Why do we have dreams? These are only some of the questions that people often ask when it comes to the topic of dreams. Wouldn't you like to know the meaning of your dreams?

In reality, not all of your dreams need to be mysteries for you to solve, and anyone can certainly acquire the ability to understand their dream's meanings. Here is a book that will guide you in interpreting your dreams. With five hundred dream symbols, this book can be a powerful tool in unlocking man's most common dreams. It contains keywords related to your dreams and their interpretations.

However, you need to know that only you have the power to truly understand the meaning of your dreams. This book will only serve as your guide as you look into how your dreams can be connected to your hidden feelings, deep secrets, your relationships with people around you, and how you live your daily life.

Dreams can have different meanings for every person. There is really no definite interpretation for one person's every dream. With this book, you will be able to have a general understanding of the most common dreams that people have. Hopefully, with this knowledge, you will be able to acquire the ability to understand your own dreams.

- A -

Abandonment

To dream of being abandoned signifies your fear of being betrayed or deserted by someone you trust. People often dream of being abandoned when a death occurs in the family. To dream of abandoning someone or something could mean that you want to be free of something that is overwhelming you.

Abduction

To dream that you are abducted or see someone being abducted signifies your feeling of powerlessness in your life. Dreams where you are abducting someone, on the other hand, mean that you are being too controlling of people around you.

Abortion

Abortion dreams signify your fear of moving forward. You may be afraid of making changes to your present situation.

Abuse

To dream of being abused signifies feelings of being taken advantage of, victimized, suppressed, and an inability to express oneself.

Abyss

To dream of falling into an abyss represents your fear of changes—the unknown and the unfamiliar. It could also signify sadness or depression.

Accident

To dream of being in an accident or witnessing an accident denotes your inability to control your present situation. Accident dreams can also occur right after experiencing a real-life accident.

Achievement

To dream of attaining a goal or winning a prize denotes your desire to experience satisfaction.

Adultery

To dream of committing adultery denotes unmet sexual needs. It could also signify a longing to be free from your present relationship. Conversely, a dream where your partner commits adultery suggests a fear of betrayal or emotional insecurities.

Afterlife

To dream that you have died and are living in an afterlife can mean that you have a desire to leave your present life behind and start a new one.

Age

To dream that you are older signifies an optimistic approach to your future. To dream about your childhood can mean unresolved issues.

Aggression

To dream of being aggressive can indicate your desire to be more assertive in your decisions. To dream of being in an aggressive situation denotes conflict that you may be experiencing with someone.

Agony

To dream of experiencing agony implies your need to face issues that you have been running away from.

Airplane

To see a plane crash in your dream signifies your fear of losing control. To dream that you are inside a smooth flight denotes your complete control of life. It can also represent your high expectations. To dream that you are about to ride an airplane signifies your desire to leave the past and move forward.

Aliens

To see aliens in your dream generally denotes a recent change in your life. Alien invasion denotes anxiousness over meeting and dealing with new people.

Alone

If in your dream, you are happy to be alone, then it signifies your need for privacy and solitude. To dream of sadness and being alone signifies the fear of rejection.

Amnesia

To dream that you have amnesia signifies your wish to forget unpleasant events and experiences.

Anger

To dream of being angry denotes containing suppressed anger. It signifies your inability to express anger in a recent experience.

Apologize

To dream of apologizing denotes a desire for conflict-free relationships. To dream that someone is apologizing to you signifies that you want someone to own up to their misdoings.

Approval

To dream about seeking approval denotes your dependency problems. To see something being approved means a longing for better circumstances. To dream about approving something denotes your positive attitude towards the future.

Ax

To dream that you are holding an ax represents negative thoughts. It could be a symbol of your intentions to hurt someone.

- B -

Baby

To dream of babies signifies new beginnings. Dropping a baby in your dream could mean a missed opportunity. A crying baby denotes the need for care and attention.

Balloon

To dream of balloons flying away from you signifies disappointments. If balloons are descending or are colored black, it denotes sadness and depression.

Bad Breath

To dream that you have bad breath signifies your lack of confidence in expressing yourself verbally. It also denotes that you need to put more thought on the things you say.

Balance

To dream of losing balance indicates a person's inability to weigh his options. It also signifies lack of stability.

Bankrupt

To dream of bankruptcy denotes a fear of losing something very important in your life. It also represents putting too much importance on money.

Beach

To dream that you are relaxing in the beach signifies your calm state of mind. If you see tumultuous waves, it indicates worries that you might have.

Beautiful

To dream of something or someone extraordinarily beautiful signifies your desire for a happy, contended life.

Bet

To dream that you are making a bet denotes the risks that you are facing. Losing in a bet denotes regrets.

Birthday

To dream of a birthday celebration denotes your desire to see or be with family and friends. It also means acceptance of oneself.

Blind, Eye Patch, Black Eye

To dream that you have a black eye, an eye patch, or blindness signifies your inability to see things the way they really are. You could be in denial about something in your life.

Boss

To dream about your boss can signify anything about your work. It could also mean your desire for a promotion.

Bride

To dream that you are a bride indicates your desire to have a long-term relationship with someone. It could be a business relationship, friendship, or a romantic relationship.

Bruise

To dream of bruises signifies painful emotions that you have suppressed. Bruises denote any kind of pain that you might be experiencing.

Brush

To dream about a scrubbing brush denotes a desire clean something up. It could also represent an intention to make a wrong right.

Bubbles

To dream about bubbles signify unrealistic expectations. It could also be a warning for a disappointment.

Bubblegum

To dream about bubblegum signifies close family ties. It also represents your ability to maintain friendships and good working relationships.

Bull's Eye

To see a bull's eye in your dream denotes that you may be right about a suspicion that you are having.

Burn

To see something burning in your dream signifies passion and romance.

Burst

To see something burst in your dream connotes that your patience is running out and you are just about to explode.

Buy

To dream that you are buying something denotes willingness to accept someone or something new. It could also represent you readiness to replace some old but well-loved things.

- C -

Cage

A cage dream signifies restrictions. To dream that you or an animal is caged denotes your lack of freedom to do the things you want.

Cancer

To dream that you have cancer signifies your feeling of hopelessness. It represents a negative outlook in life and your choice to just give up on everything.

Cancellation

To dream that an appointment or a flight was cancelled denotes a fear to confront something that is bothering you.

Cat

To dream of a cat denotes your desire to be free from boundaries, to come and go as you please, and to be mysterious. It also denotes sexuality.

Casket

To dream that you are inside a coffin signifies being in a controlling relationship. It indicates your need to break-up with this person.

Castration

To dream of castration denotes your fear of impotence. It also represents your powerlessness about a situation.

Captive

To dream that you are a captive denotes your dissatisfaction with your career, relationship, or present situation.

Car

To dream that you are driving a car represents your ability to take full control of your life. Any car problem means that you need to slow down and think things through.

Cave

To dream that you are in a cave denotes your need to do some self-reflection. It could also denote feelings of being in a dark place.

Centaur

To dream of a centaur denotes a mix-up or confusion about an issue. It could mean that you are unable to make a clear decision about something.

Christening

To dream that you are in a christening ceremony denotes a yearning for a fresh start. It also means purity and innocence.

Christmas Tree

To dream about a Christmas tree denotes feelings of wanting to buy a home. It can also signify a desire to start a family.

Cigar, Cigarette

To dream that you are smoking a cigar or a cigarette when you are not a smoker signifies that you might be considering smoking. It could also denote bad habits that you need to stop doing. It can also have something to do with the need to explore certain aspects of your sexuality.

Circus

To dream about the circus signifies your life's lack of order. It could also represent your emotional and mental health.

Coloring Book

To dream that you are coloring a book signifies that you have an active role in how your life will turn out. You have clear plans and you know exactly what to do. To watch someone else coloring denotes a passive role that you are taking.

Coma

To dream that you are in a coma denotes powerlessness. To see your body in a coma denotes separating yourself from reality.

Crash

To dream about a crash signifies pessimism. You may be expecting or wishing that something will go wrong.

Cremation

To dream about a cremation denotes your desire to let go of the past and have a fresh start.

Crystal Ball

To dream about a crystal ball signifies your need for advice, guidance, and support from family and friends.

Cyclone

To dream about a cyclone denotes an inner turmoil. The dream represents repressed emotions that may be coming up to the surface.

- D -

Dance

To dream of dancing signifies happiness, contentment, freedom from boundaries, and self-acceptance.

Danger

Dreams of danger denote feelings of uncertainty and anxiousness. It can also signify apprehension for an impending change.

Darkness

To dream of being engulfed in darkness signifies a person's ignorance and failures. A light breaking into the darkness can mean hope and a possibility for success and happiness.

Death

To dream of a person who has passed away signifies that you miss the person, would like to say your final goodbye, or that you are still coping with your loss. To dream that you are dead can mean that you'd like to escape your present situation.

Dead End

To dream of a dead end signifies giving up. It could also represent a dead end job or a relationship that is not working.

Deadline

To dream about deadlines represent your feelings of inadequacy and panic that you have not yet accomplished the goals you have.

Debt

To dream about debt signifies your financial worries. If in your dream, you are lending money to others, it denotes your willingness to help. A dream about a debt can also pertain to favors that you have done for other people and vice versa.

Devil

To dream about the devil represents feelings of guilt. It also denotes possible temptations around you.

Ditch

Seeing a ditch in your dream can be a symbol that you need to be wary of someone. It is a warning that you need to be careful.

Diving

To dream that you are diving denotes your desire to understand an issue in your life. It also signifies your confidence.

Doppelganger

To see a look-alike in your dream signifies an inner conflict. It could also point to how you accept all aspects of your person or individuality.

Drowning

To dream that you are drowning denotes your feelings of being overwhelmed. It could symbolize your deep involvement with something that you now wish to get out of.

Drunk

To dream that you are drunk signifies that you need to be more tactful about what you say and do.

Duct Tape

To dream that you are using duct tape denotes a controlling attitude. It also represents your obsession to keep things intact.

Duel

To dream about a duel signifies your readiness to fight for what you want. It can also mean determination and persistence.

Duet

To dream that you are singing a duet signifies acceptance of self. It denotes harmony and cooperation.

Dummy

To see a dummy in your dream signifies the lack of excitement in your life. It also represents boredom due to the lack of new challenges and opportunities for growth.

Dungeon

To dream that you are in a dungeon signifies work-related frustration. You may be wishing that you had access to much more modern equipment.

Dyeing

To dream that you are dyeing your hair or someone else's hair denotes a yearning for someone else's life.

Dynamite

To dream about dynamites signifies danger. It could also be a warning about making someone angry.

- E -

Earthquake

To dream of an earthquake represents your fears for a major change happening in your career or in your relationships.

Eating

To dream that you are eating denotes survival instincts. To dream that you are eating with your family signifies happiness, love, and contentment.

Eavesdropping

To dream that you are eavesdropping signifies insecurity and low self-esteem. It also implies that you are overly suspicious of the people around you.

Education

To dream about studying, enrolling, or going to school signifies your yearning for knowledge.

Ejaculation

To dream that you have ejaculated signifies your desire to express yourself more freely. It could represent your intention to be more verbal about your ideas and feelings.

Embarrassment

To dream that you are in an embarrassing situation denotes your insecurities. These dreams often occur before speeches and presentations.

Enemy

To dream of an adversary or a rival can mean that you have conflicting ideas or emotions. There could also be a real life rival that is posing as a threat you.

Engagement

To dream that you are engaged to be married signifies a desire for a stable romantic relationship. A broken engagement can mean uncertainty over decisions you've made.

Escape

To dream of escaping signifies your readiness to leave behind the past. It also symbolizes a good future. To dream about escaping also denotes your yearning for a new job and a new life.

Eulogy

To dream that you are giving a eulogy at a funeral signifies repressed thoughts and emotions. To dream that you are listening to someone give a eulogy signifies that you need to listen.

Ex-Boyfriend, Ex-Girlfriend

To dream of an ex signifies dissatisfaction in your present-day life. It represents feelings that you may still have for an ex-flame. Also, you may be remembering a time in your life when you were much happier.

Euthanasia

To dream of euthanasia denotes your desire to have more control of your life. It signifies your need to make decisions for yourself and to have the ability to support yourself financially.

Explosion

To witness an explosion in your dream signifies anger that you have not expressed.

Exit

To see the 'Exit' sign or to look for it in your dream signifies your desire to try new things. It also represents a way out of your present situation.

Eyesight

To have vision problems in your dream denotes your inability to make strong and clear decisions.

- F -

Faceless

To dream that you are faceless denotes identity issues. You may not be sure yet of who you really are. To see a faceless person means that you are not yet familiar with this person.

Facelift

To dream that you had a facelift signifies your desire to make changes in your life.

Failure

To dream of failing signifies your worries and insecurities. It could also be a reflection of your lack of self-confidence. On the other hand, a dream about failing can provide insights on how to prevent the failure.

Fair

To dream that you are in a fair denotes your longing for better circumstances. It could also mean that you wish your life was simpler.

Fake

To discover that something is fake in your dream denotes that something or someone in your life is not what it seems. It could also mean that you are not being true to your feelings.

Falling

To dream of falling signifies your fears of failure. It could also represent a big problem that you are having at the moment.

Fame

To dream that you are famous signifies your need to be praised and get the approval of others. If in your dream you are in the company of famous people, it denotes success and good fortune.

Family

To dream of your family in a loving environment represents security and stability. The opposite denotes family troubles.

Fat

To dream that you are fat denotes good fortune and success in your career. It symbolizes prosperity, good health, and money.

Father

To dream of your father signifies your longing for financial security. It could also represent goals that you want to achieve. To dream that you are a small child and you are with your father denotes fears that you might not measure up to your parent when you become a father yourself.

Film

To dream that you are filming signifies your desire to preserve all the good memories in your life. Conversely, to dream that someone else is filming you signifies your trust and appreciation for people that care for you.

Finish Line

To see the finish line in your dream could signify the accomplishment of your goals. It could also be an ominous warning that your end is near.

Flying

To dream of flying denotes a newly found freedom. It could also represent confidence.

Forgive

To dream that you are asking forgiveness or that someone is asking for your forgiveness signifies your desire for a conflict-free environment.

Fur

To dream about fur denotes vanity and the love for all expensive and luxurious things. This dream can also be a symbol for warmth and comfort.

- G -

Gagging

To gag or choke in your dream denotes that you are not being honest to yourself and to other people. It could also mean that you are worried about something that you've said and now wish that you have kept your mouth shut.

Game Show

To be a contestant in a game show in your dream denotes your need to be a part of something big. To be an audience member in a game show denotes that you are satisfied with where you are right now.

Gang

To dream that you are a member of a gang represents your need to belong. To dream that you're being attacked by a gang signifies you being unprepared for a big change happening in your life.

Giraffe

To dream of a giraffe signifies that you want to be recognized and looked up to. It represents high ambition.

Gnome

Gnome dreams represent good luck, prosperity, and fertility. It could also represent your childhood.

Goodbye

To dream that you are saying goodbye to someone signifies new prospects and better opportunities. To dream that someone bids you farewell denotes your acceptance of things.

Gossip

Gossiping in your dream denotes your lack of awareness of the truth. You need to find out what's really happening around you.

Grapes

Eating grapes in your dream symbolizes wealth, fame, and success. It also means fertility and long life.

Grave

To see a grave in your dream denotes unpleasant issues in your life that you need to face.

Groceries

To dream of groceries denote your need for fulfillment. Groceries represent all the things that you feel you are lacking in your life.

Guilt

To feel guilty in your dream denotes low self-esteem. You feel that you don't deserve the good things in your life.

Gun

Guns represent anger or an imminent danger to you. When a gun is fired, it means fertility and fruitfulness, but if it misfires, it could symbolize impotence.

Gypsy

To dream that you are a gypsy signifies your desire to be able to freely express yourself verbally, emotionally, mentally, spiritually, and physically.

- H -

Hacking

To dream that you are accessing someone else's computer illegally denotes your lack of sense for boundaries. You may be intruding on other people's privacy.

Hail

To dream of hail signifies troubled times. It could also mean negative emotions, sadness, and depression.

Hair

To dream that you have long hair means fertility and good career. To dream that you are cutting your hair denotes the need for change, and to dream that you have gray hair signifies your fear of growing old.

Heart

To see a heart in your dream signifies your romantic life. A healthy heart denotes a fulfilling relationship and a bleeding heart denotes a troubled one.

Heart Attack

To have a heart attack in your dream denotes your lack of control over your life. It could also mean that you are feeling threatened by someone.

Height

To be at a very high place such as the top of a mountain or a building means achievement of your goals. To be afraid of heights in your dream could mean that the goals you have set for yourself are too high.

Hell

To dream of hell connotes very unsatisfying circumstances. You may feel that your situation is at its worst.

Help

To dream that you are asking for help can be a real cry for help. Do some self-reflection and don't be afraid to ask for help and support from professionals, family, and friends.

Hiding

To dream that you are hiding signifies that you are not ready for something. To see someone hiding in your dream could mean that you are uncomfortable around this person.

High Heels

To dream that you are wearing high heels denote big responsibilities. A broken heel symbolizes hardship in taking on these duties. To dream that you are walking in high heels with no discomfort whatsoever denotes that you are capable.

Hole

To see a hole in your dream represents unfulfilled dreams. It could also symbolize dissatisfaction with your life.

Homosexual

To dream that you are a homosexual signifies your desire to travel, see new sights, and experience something new.

Horseshoe

To dream about a horseshow signifies a forthcoming wedding. It also connotes luck and good health.

Hotel

To dream that you are staying at a hotel denotes your adventurous side and a desire to break free from your daily routine.

- I -

Iceberg

To dream of an iceberg signifies that you are intimidated by a person of authority. You long to 'break the ice' with this person but are unable to.

Identification

To dream about your I.D. signifies your self-confidence. It also connotes that you have definite and clear plans for your future. To lose your I.D. means you are uncertain about your future.

Ignore

To dream that you are being ignored means you need to open your eyes to the reality around you. To dream that you are ignoring someone signifies a past that you'd rather forget.

Illness

To dream of being ill means that you are very unhappy about your situation. It could also mean loss of hope.

Impotence

To dream that you are unable to perform sexually connotes your feeling of powerlessness. It could also signify insecurities when it comes to your sexual prowess.

Immobile

To dream that you cannot move represents your fear of commitment and long-term relationships.

Incest

To dream of incest signifies an inner conflict. You may be going through a life-changing event and are unable to cope with it.

Independent

To dream that you are independent denotes freedom, happiness, and contentment. It also means that you have a very high regard for your abilities.

Injury

To dream of being injured denotes the grudges you are holding and also thoughts of revenge.

Interrogation

To dream of being interrogated denotes your distaste for someone who is overbearing. It represents your feeling of being bullied.

Intersection

To see an intersection in your dream connotes the decisions that you have to make.

Intoxication

To dream that you are drunk signifies your need to unwind and break free from common social restrictions.

Invisible

To dream that you are invisible represents your feelings of being ignored and unnoticed. It represents your desire to be acknowledged and recognized.

- J -

Jack-in-the-Box

To dream about this toy connotes life's surprises. New things might be coming to your life.

Jack O' Lantern

To dream about a Jack O' Lantern signifies toughness, determination, and your ability to face anything that is coming right at you.

Jacket

To dream about a jacket denotes a need to protect yourself from people around you. The jacket represents a shield that you use so that society cannot harm you.

Jacuzzi

Relaxing in a hot tub in your dream denotes your desire to be true to yourself. It also symbolizes recklessness and wantonness.

Jade

To dream of wearing jade signifies happiness, luck, prosperity, and success. To dream that someone gives you jade means that you are loved.

Jaguar

To dream of a Jaguar signifies a new love. It could also mean problems at the workplace.

Jealousy

Dreams of being jealous represent your lack of trust for the people around you. To dream that people are jealous of you denotes your high self-esteem.

Jester

To see a jester in your dream represents the happy moments in your life. To dream about a scary jester denotes unresolved family issues.

Jewelry

To dream that someone gives you jewelry signifies your belief in your abilities. To dream about a broken jewelry represents disappointments.

Journey

To dream about going on a journey signifies self-discovery. It also denotes new challenges coming your way.

Judge

To dream about a judge denotes remorse. It also represents your feeling that people are judging you.

Juggling

To dream about juggling denotes feelings of being overwhelmed with too many things. It also symbolizes your inability to accept that you can't handle too many responsibilities.

Jungle

To dream that you are in a jungle signifies disorder. It denotes feelings of being lost and disoriented.

Jupiter

To dream about the planet Jupiter denotes expansion, development, and growth.

Justice

To dream about justice being served symbolizes your belief in the justice system.

- K -

Kaleidoscope

To see a kaleidoscope in your dream signifies self-reflection. It denotes your ability to learn from past experiences.

Kangaroo

Kangaroo dreams represent motherhood. You may also be missing your mother. A jumping kangaroo denotes a fear of commitment.

Karaoke

To dream that you are singing in a karaoke bar denotes taking control of your life. It represents confidence in yourself and in your abilities.

Karate

To dream that you know karate signifies your desire to stand up for yourself.

Karma

To dream about karma signifies strong beliefs for justice. It represents your feelings for moral righteousness.

Key

To dream about a key denotes new opportunities. Losing a key in your dream means misses opportunities and lack of self-confidence.

Kill

To dream about killing someone denotes your need to break free from your restrictions. To be killed in your dream means that you have trouble accepting some aspects of yourself.

Kindergarten

To dream about your kindergarten years signify unresolved emotions. It also means that you are seeking comfort from your childhood days.

Kiss

To dream that you are kissing or being kissed by someone signifies happiness, contentment, harmony, and satisfaction.

Kite

To dream of a kite signifies a lost love or some far away dream that you refuse to let go. It could also mean feelings of being controlled and manipulated.

Kneel

To dream that you are kneeling denotes humility. To dream that someone is kneeling before you signifies your pride and yearning for redemption.

Knife

When a man dreams about a knife, it signifies his sexual prowess. When a woman dreams about a knife, it means that she has unfulfilled sexual needs.

Knocking

To dream that someone is knocking on your door denotes that someone needs your attention. To dream that you are knocking signifies plans of visiting someone.

Knots

To dream about knots denote possible confrontations with your boss or a family member. To see a single knot in your dream signifies an upcoming wedding.

Koala

To dream about a koala signifies places of comfort such as your parents' house, a family cabin, or your own apartment.

- L -

Labyrinth

To dream that you are inside a labyrinth represents your confusion about something in your life. It could also mean a desire to change your career.

Ladder

A ladder in your dream symbolizes a way out. It is a symbol of hope. The absence of a ladder from where it should be denotes feelings of being trapped and restrained.

Lace

To dream about lace signifies a wedding. For a man, it can also mean getting in touch with your feminine side.

Lactation

To dream that you are lactating denotes a desire to be a parent. It also symbolizes your relationship with your mother.

Lamb

To dream about a lamb represents your fear that someone is deceiving you. The lamb could also be a symbol of your helplessness or powerlessness.

Laughing

To see yourself laughing in your dream symbolizes your positive attitude. To hear a scary, demonic laugh symbolizes feelings of inadequacy.

Leaving

To dream that you or someone else is leaving connotes readiness for new things. It could also mean willingness to forgive and forget.

Legs

To dream that you have good legs signify your confidence that your life is in order and that you can support yourself effectively. To dream of wounded, deformed legs or missing limbs denote fears about your future.

Letters

To see letters in your dream signify that you need to communicate better with those around you.

Levitation

To dream that you are levitating denotes a promotion. To dream that you can make things levitate signifies that your intelligence and skill will someday make you into a powerful person.

Lightning

To see lighting in your dream suggests a need to broaden your knowledge. To be struck with lighting in your dream denotes your inability to accept new information that you have heard.

Limousine

To dream that you are riding in a limo signifies success and fame.

Listen

To dream that you are listening to something denotes an interest to learn. To dream that you are talking but no one seems to be listening denotes a lack of confidence in your capabilities.

Lock

To dream about a lock denotes a relationship that is going nowhere. It can also symbolize a dead-end job.

Lust

To dream about lust symbolizes your need to get what you want. It also represents high goals.

- M -

Madness

To dream that you are mad signifies an overwhelming feeling that you cannot cope with life's challenges. These dreams also occur after a death, a tragic accident, separation, loss of a job, or bankruptcy.

Magic

To dream of magic denotes a longing to escape your reality. It could also denote false hope. To dream that you are capable of doing magic signifies your desire to have skills and abilities that are much more than what you are capable of.

Makeup

To dream about putting on makeup signifies a desire to improve your present circumstances. It could also symbolize the need to put on a face or to exercise caution with your words and actions.

Making Out

To dream that you are making out with someone denotes a secret desire for this person. It could also mean that you just need to listen and give this person a chance.

Mask

To dream that you have a mask on denotes your unwillingness to show your true personality. To be in a masquerade ball represents your fear that people aren't being true to you.

Masochism

To dream that you are a masochist signifies unhappiness with your work or relationships.

Masturbation

To dream that you are masturbating denotes that you have a strong will and determination to achieve your goals. It symbolizes that you are not afraid to exert a little effort to get what you really want.

Midget

To dream about a midget symbolizes feelings of insecurity. It also represents a feeling that you are unable to compete with your colleagues.

Mirror

To dream about you looking into a mirror symbolizes self-acceptance. A broken, cracked, foggy, dirty mirror represents confusion, uncertainty, and bad luck.

Mistress

To dream that your husband has a mistress represents your low self-esteem. To dream that you are a mistress signifies your desire for financial security.

Morgue

To dream that you are in a morgue signifies a fear that you might not achieve your goals while you are alive.

Morning

To dream that it is morning signifies a renewal, a fresh start, and a chance to make things better.

Mortgage

To dream about your mortgage denotes financial worries. It can also signify a separation or a divorce.

Motel

To dream that you are in a motel signifies a transitional phase in your life. It could also mean that you are happy with the lack of permanence in your life.

Murder

To dream about murder signifies that a part of your life has come to an end. It could symbolize the end of a phase.

- N -

Nag

To dream that you are nagging represents a feeling that people aren't listening to you and that you are not being taken seriously. To see someone nagging symbolizes that you need to make better decisions in life.

Naked

To dream that you are naked represents your feelings of vulnerability. It could also mean that you are keeping a secret that you don't want people to find out. However, if your nakedness does not bother you in your dream, then it symbolizes your confidence.

Name

To dream about someone calling your name denotes a desire to be accepted and recognized. To dream about forgetting your name or another person's name signifies an identity crisis or an inner conflict.

Narrow

To find yourself in narrow spaces in your dream signify your lack of options. It can also represent your inability to think out of the box.

Near-Death Experience

To dream that you were in a near-death experience symbolizes a grave situation that you were able to overcome.

Net

To dream about a net signifies the expansion of business connections. To dream that you have fallen but were caught in a net denotes financial and emotional security.

Ninja

To dream about a ninja signifies a person's need for privacy and solitude. You may be feeling overwhelmed with the company of people and would just like to have some private time.

Night

To dream that it is night signifies a need to rest. It is also a symbol of protection and safety.

Nipples

To dream that your nipples are exposed denotes vulnerability. It could also signify your fear of being exposed.

Nose

To dream about your nose denotes distrust, suspicion, and caution. It could also mean that you need to butt out of other people's businesses.

Notebook

To dream that you are writing or reading from a notebook signifies your excitement for upcoming events.

Numbers

Dreams about numbers represent money, good fortune, fertility, and productivity.

Nun

To dream that you are nun when you are not one in real life signifies a desire for simple living. A dream about a nun also denotes spirituality.

Nurse

To dream of a nurse denotes your yearning for someone to care for you.

Nymph

To dream about a nymph signifies a woman that you find desirable.

- O -

Oak

To dream of oak signifies strength, endurance, tolerance, and determination.

Obedience

To dream that you are obeying someone signifies your respect for your boss. To disobey in your dream denotes a conflict between you and the management.

Oasis

To dream about an oasis signifies your need to be 'saved' from your circumstances. It could also mean that better things are coming your way.

Obituary

To dream that you are reading an obituary denotes your regrets in life.

Obscene

A dream about obscenity represents your inhibitions and reservations. You may be longing to express yourself more.

Octopus

To dream about an octopus denotes infidelity. It can also be a symbol for polygamy.

Ogre

To dream about an ogre signifies your sudden realization about the ugly side of something.

Operator

To dream about an operator denotes that someone is there to help you.

Oral Sex

To dream that you are giving oral sex signifies good communication skills. To dream that you are receiving oral sex denotes that you need to listen more to other people.

Orangutan

To dream about an orangutan denotes sexual abandon. It also symbolizes primal needs.

Orchard

A dream about an orchard symbolizes fertility, productivity, fruitfulness, and success.

Orgasm

To dream about having an orgasm signifies satisfaction with your life. Inability to reach orgasm in your dream connotes dissatisfaction.

Outer Space

To dream of outer space connotes open-mindedness, freedom, and endless possibilities.

Oven

To have a dream that you are cooking something in the oven denotes pregnancy, new ideas, a new business, or a new love.

Owl

To dream of an owl denotes a bad omen, death, and ill fortune. It could also signify a newfound wisdom.

- P -

Package

To dream about a package denotes your untapped potentials. It also means that a surprise is in store for you.

Pageant

To dream that you are a contestant in a pageant signifies worries about being judged. To win in a pageant means you have overcome your fears.

Pain

To dream that you are experiencing pain denotes overworking. It also means that you need to relax and take things easy.

Pawnshop

To dream that you are inside a pawnshop represents your financial worries.

Peep

To dream that you are peeping or that someone is peeping on you connotes mistrust. It represents your lack of confidence in your capabilities or in other people's.

Perm

To dream about getting a perm denotes a willingness to see things from another point of view.

Picture

To dream about pictures represent the desire for permanency, stability, and commitment.

Poison

To dream about poison connotes harmful thoughts you might be entertaining. It also means that there are people around you that you need to cut ties with.

Poor

To dream about poverty denotes hopelessness, lack of ambition, and negativity.

Pregnant

To dream about pregnancy signifies career development. It also means that your hard work is finally bearing fruits.

Psychopath

To dream about a psychopath signifies fear of losing control. It also means that you want to try out things that you would not normally want to do.

Pub

To dream that you are in a pub signifies friendship and socializing. It also symbolizes the need to unwind.

Public Speaking

To dream that you are speaking in front of a large crowd but you are not a public speaker in real life signifies an ambition to run for political office. It also connotes reaching a high position in a company.

Pulling

To dream that you are pulling someone denotes a need to influence a person to your thinking. To dream that you are being pulled signifies your openness to new ideas.

Pursuit

To dream that you are in pursuit of something or someone denotes your efforts to attain your goals. To dream that someone is in pursuit of you signifies possible options that you have not considered.

- Q -

Quadruplets

A dream about quadruplets represents numerous career opportunities. It is also a reminder that there is more than one way of doing things.

Quail

To dream about a quail signifies feelings of being small. Nevertheless, you feel that you can face any kind of challenge that life throws at you.

Quarrel

To have a quarrel with someone in your dream connotes your desire to be more honest with your feelings.

Queen

To dream that you are a queen represents a need to be treated better by your husband. It could also represent your suspicions that a man you know is gay.

Quest

To dream that you are in a quest for something denotes unfulfilled desires and longings for love, stability, wealth, and happiness.

Question

To dream that you are asking a question or that someone is asking you a question denotes your uncertainty and lack of direction.

Quicksand

To dream that you, an animal, or someone else is sinking in quicksand represents your fear that the decision you recently made might be wrong.

Quiet

To dream that your surroundings are quiet represents your yearning for cooperation, harmony, and peace.

Quilt

To dream of a quilt signifies good relationships within your family. It also means that you are comfortable about where you are now.

Quiz

To dream about taking a quiz denotes your fear of being criticized and judged.

- R -

Rabbit

To dream about a rabbit denotes a happy sex life. It also means fertility and children.

Race

To dream that you are in a race signifies that you are running out of time. It could also mean that you are rushing into things too soon.

Raffle

To dream of a raffle signifies unemployment and lack of financial stability. It can also symbolize too much dependence on fate.

Raft

To dream that you are riding a raft denotes temporary relief or a false sense of security.

Rage

To dream that you are in rage represents your need to express your anger more in your waking life.

Rape

To dream that you are raped denotes your hateful feelings of being intruded upon and the lack of respect for your privacy. To see your daughter being raped signifies your anxiety about your children becoming more independent.

Recurring Dream

To have the same dream denotes that you have some unfinished business and issues that you need to resolve.

Rehearsal

To dream that you are in a rehearsal denotes preparation. Your dream is telling you that you need to get ready for something.

Remarry

To dream that you are getting married again symbolizes a second chance for you. It also connotes that you are willing to give something a second try.

Repair

To dream that you are repairing something denotes recuperating from physical or emotional wounds. It can also mean standing up after a fall.

Reputation

To dream that you are concerned for your reputation or someone else's denotes the fears of rejection and being criticized or judged by other people.

Ring

To see a ring in your dream denotes long-term commitments, stability, and security.

River

To dream about a river signifies your lack of control over your life. It also denotes the need to take ahold of your life.

Road Trip

To dream that you are on a road trip signifies that you need to take things slowly. It also means that you need to be careful about decisions you make and roads you take.

Running

Running in your dream denotes avoidance of conflict and urgent matters.

- S -

Sad

To dream about being sad connotes a problem in your life that you need to resolve.

Sadism

To dream that you are a sadist signifies your lack of concern for the well-being of the people around you.

Safe

To dream about a safe or about being safe connotes emotional, mental, spiritual, and financial stability.

Sailing

To dream about sailing signifies your life. Your dream can tell you whether you are the captain of your own boat or not and whether you are sailing in smooth waters or you're having some trouble controlling your boat.

Salary

To dream that you have a high salary denotes self-confidence and to dream that you have a low salary symbolizes your low self-esteem.

Secret Admirer

To dream about having a secret admirer denotes your need to be accepted. To dream that you are secretly admiring someone signifies a desire to model yourself after this person.

Self-Defense

To dream of self-defense symbolizes your feeling of being threatened or bullied. It can also mean that you can stand up for yourself when push comes to shove.

Sex

To dream that you are having sex denotes your desire to express yourself verbally, intellectually, and physically.

Seasons

To dream about any season denotes level-headedness and a sense of being grounded. To dream about seasons changing right before your eyes symbolizes worries that you might be having about your children and husband/wife.

Shame

To dream that you are ashamed signifies hidden secrets that are in danger of coming out.

Sinking, Sinkhole

To dream about a sinkhole or that you are sinking denotes despair. It also symbolizes your feeling that someone or something is pulling you back.

Skydiving

To dream that you are skydiving represents high expectations and ideals. It can also symbolize unrealistic goals.

Spiders

To dream of a spider symbolizes a female who has a big influence in your life—your mother, female boss, or wife.

Stranger

To dream about a person that you've never met or seen before denotes aspects of yourself that you've kept repressed. It may be time to acknowledge this part of yourself.

Surprise

To dream that you are surprised signifies that you are not afraid of the future and that you are prepared for it.

- T -

Tail

To dream that you have a tail signifies new relationships. It also denotes learning a new skill or advancement in your career.

Talent Show

To dream that you are participating in a talent show signifies that you are becoming aware of your own skills and capabilities. It could also mean the opposite where you are in doubt your skills.

Talk Show

To dream that you are a guest in a talk show denotes your need to open up about an experience. It also signifies your longing for someone who you can really talk to and a person who will listen and understand you.

Tap Dancing

To dream that you are tap dancing denotes that you are moving through your life too fast. Your dream could be telling you that you need to take a breath and slow down.

Tattoo

To dream about a tattoo symbolizes an influential person or someone that you can't easily forget. It can also represent ideals and beliefs that are hard to shake.

Teacher

To dream about an old teacher signifies a desire to go back to school. To dream that you are teaching a class denotes your need to share your skills and knowledge.

Teeth

Dreams about teeth generally symbolize a person's communication skills or the lack of it. To dream about good teeth mean that the person has great communication skills and to dream of rotting or falling teeth denotes the need to be more careful about what you say.

Theater

To dream that you are watching something in the theater denotes self-reflection. It signifies looking back at your life and what you've made of it.

Thin

To dream that you are thinner than your present self signifies personal problems that are slowly getting to you. You need to find solutions quickly.

Tired

To dream that you are tired signifies your need to move on with your life. It denotes holding on to emotions or people that are harmful to you.

Tombstone

To see your tombstone in your dream may be a representation of your fear of death. It also symbolizes your need to finish something before it's too late.

Tornado

To dream about a tornado symbolizes chaos in your life. You may have to rearrange, organize, and put some things in order.

Tourist

To dream that you are a tourist signifies unfamiliarity or the lack of knowledge about something. It means that you are experiencing something new to you.

Trousers

To dream that you forgot to put on your trousers denotes your desire to take a break from your role as the breadwinner. It could also mean that you long for a life that is free of obligations and responsibilities.

Tug-of-War

To dream that you are in a tug-of-war signifies your need to be in control and in the right. It also means that you are unwilling to listen to other people.

- U -

U-Turn

To dream about a U-turn signifies regretting about a decision you've made. It can also symbolize a chance to turn back and correct a mistake.

UFO

To dream about a UFO connotes ideas that may be out of this world. It can also be a reminder for you to keep your feet on the ground.

Ugly

To dream that you are ugly symbolizes vanity and the need to be beautiful in the eyes of other people. To dream about ugly things signify an upsetting situation.

Ukulele

To dream that you are playing the ukulele, but don't in real life, denotes a desire to learn new skills. Your dream might be telling you to expand your knowledge.

Ultrasound

To dream that you or someone else is getting an ultrasound denotes a desire to know more about someone whom you find very intriguing.

Umbrella

To dream that you are carrying an umbrella signifies preparedness. To forget to bring your umbrella in your dream denotes the opposite.

Underground

To dream that you are underground denotes your feelings of being unappreciated.

Underwater

To dream about the bottom of the ocean or any body of water or about being underwater signifies feelings of being overwhelmed.

Unicorn

To see a unicorn in your dream denotes fantasies that you may be entertaining.

Universe

To dream of seeing the universe signifies that you should not dwell on small things but instead see the big picture.

Unprepared

To dream that you are not ready for something symbolizes your unpreparedness in real life for new responsibilities.

Upholstery

To dream that you are repairing or changing your upholstery signifies your desire for a makeover of your physical appearance. To dream about good upholstery denotes your contentment with your looks.

Uproot

To dream that you are uprooting plants denote family problems. It could also symbolize your plans for relocation.

Urination

To dream that you are urinating signifies your need to talk to someone and open up about secret or pent-up emotions.

Urn

To dream about an urn signifies a hiding place. It can also symbolize your need for more storage space in your home.

- V -

Vacant

To dream about something vacant denotes feelings that something is missing in your life.

Vacation

To dream about going on a vacation can be an extension of your conscious thoughts. You may have been planning or longing for one.

Vaccination

To dream that you or someone else is getting a vaccine denotes sacrifices that you have to make in order to improve your current situation.

Vacuum

To dream about a vacuum denotes hollowness. It could represent your dissatisfaction with your work and romantic relationship.

Valentine's Day

To dream about Valentine's Day represents your excitement for the event. On the other hand, you could be dreading the day and it has manifested in your dream.

Valet

To dream that a valet is assisting you denotes dependency issues. It also represents your lack of ability to make your own decisions.

Vasectomy

To dream about a vasectomy represents your desire to cut someone off your life. It could also denote a bad habit that you want to kick off.

Vault

To dream about a vault connotes untapped potential. Your dream could be telling you to fully utilize your talents. A dream about a vault also represents trust.

Vegetarian

To dream that you have become vegetarian denotes a sudden change in your life. It could also signify that you need to be more conscious of your health.

Visitor

To dream that you have a visitor denotes good news coming your way. It can also mean a change of management in the company you work for.

Voices

To dream about hearing voices denote that you need to speak up about something that is bugging you. It could also mean that you should open your ears. To dream that you have lost your voice represents your lack of say over a decision.

Volcano

To dream about a volcano signifies your temper. You may have been holding on to your anger for too long.

Vomit

To dream that you are vomiting signifies your inability to accept something in your current situation. To dream of being vomited on denotes your helplessness over a bad situation happening to you right now.

Vote

To dream that you are voting signifies your desire to be part of a major decision. It also means that you want your voice to be heard.

Vow

To dream about you or other people making vows denote a yearning for more stable relationships. It can also be a symbol of you wanting to change for the better.

- W -

Wailing

To dream that you are wailing or to hear someone wailing denotes sadness and pain that you have not expressed outwardly. You need to talk to someone about how you feel.

Waiting

To dream that you are waiting for someone or something denotes that you are at a point in your life where you are not free to move forward or do something. You have no choice but to remain where you are and your next move fully depends on the person or the thing that you are 'waiting' for.

Wall

A dream about a wall has many connotations. It could be a symbol of strength and protection. It can also denote hiding and the inability to face an issue. A dream about a wall can also represent the desire for privacy.

Wagon

The appearance of a wagon in your dream symbolizes alcoholism. Your dream could be telling you that you need to cut down on liquor. If you are not a drinker, then it can represent your fear that someone you know is over-drinking.

Warning

To be warned in your dream signifies a pressing matter that you need to give your immediate attention.

Wake

To dream that you are in a wake signifies your fear of your parents dying. It means that you are not emotionally and mentally prepared for this possibility.

Wallpaper

To dream that you are putting wallpaper on your wall signifies a longing for a better life. To dream that you are stripping down old wallpaper denotes putting down your defenses and accepting change.

Walker

To dream about a child in a walker denotes hope and possibility. It can also denote learning.

Walking Stick

To dream about a walking stick represents memories of a dead grandparent. It also signifies a fear of growing old.

Weaving

To dream about weaving denotes planning. It can also symbolize manipulation and deceit.

Wheel of Fortune

To dream about a wheel of fortune signifies the risks you might be taking. It could be a warning for you to not rely too much on chance.

Wheelchair

To dream that you are in wheelchair denotes feelings of being pushed around. It also represents dependency issues.

Wig

To dream of wearing a wig denotes the parts of yourself that you are trying to hide from other people.

Wilderness

To dream that you are lost in the wilderness signifies your desire to be free and to be able to do the things you want.

Womb

To dream about a womb symbolizes comfort, warmth, safety.

Wrestling

To dream about wrestling signifies your struggle in balancing the daily aspects of your life such as your family, relationships, career, social life, etc.

- X -

X-Ray

To dream that you are getting an x-ray signifies your fear that people will see right through you. To dream that you are looking at an x-ray denotes that you have to look past people's outward appearance.

Xylophone

To dream that you or another person is playing the xylophone signifies your expectation to hear good news in the next few days.

- Y-

Yacht

To dream about a yacht symbolizes your desire to go on a luxurious vacation or just to take a break from a grueling situation.

Yard

To dream about a yard signifies that you need to give more time and attention to your family. An unkempt yard can symbolize family troubles, but a well-maintained yard can mean that all is in order.

Yard Sale

To dream that you are in a yard sale denotes your need to pay attention to the things that matter. It can mean that you shouldn't discard stuff or disregard people that are really important in your life.

Yes

To dream about the word "yes" signifies a positive turn of events. It could also be a representation of your desire for things to turn out the way you want.

Yesterday

To dream about event that happened the previous day denotes that you may be missing something. You need to be more attentive to what's happening around you.

Yin-Yang

To dream about the Yin-Yang signifies your need for balance. There might be aspects of your life that are out of balance.

Yoga

To dream that you are doing yoga or watching other people doing yoga signifies your need adjust to changes and to be more flexible.

Yolk

To dream about an egg yolk signifies a new life. It could also symbolize new opportunities.

Young

To dream that you or someone else is young again may be a reminder that you should not forget favors that people have done for you in the past.

Yoyo

To dream about a yo-yo denotes regression. Your dream could be a warning that you are going back instead of moving forward.

- Z -

Zebra

To see a zebra in your dream signifies that you need to be more flexible and stop seeing things in just black and white.

Zenith

To dream of a zenith denotes hope that something good is out there waiting for you.

Zephyr

To dream about a zephyr signifies high goals. It could also be a symbol for a relaxed, comfortable life.

Zero

To dream about the number zero symbolizes continuity. It can also represent a person from your past who is resurfacing in your life.

Zigzag

To dream about a zigzag denotes abrupt, possibly thoughtless or rash decisions. It can also signify sudden changes.

Zinnias

To see Zinnias in your dream signifies a summer fling or fun summertime memories.

Zip Code

To dream about your zip code signifies stability. To dream about another zip code could represent plans for moving.

Zip Line

To dream about riding a zip line denotes your desire for adventure. Your dream could also be telling you that you need to enjoy life more.

Zipper

To dream that your zipper gets stuck signifies a bad romantic or business relationship.

Zombie

To dream that you are a zombie denotes physical and mental exhaustion. To dream that zombies are after you represents your disgust for people who take advantage of you.

Zoo

To dream that you are in a zoo looking at caged animals signifies your unhappiness with the company you work for. To dream that you are one of the animals in the zoo represents your dependence to your job.

Post Script

Understanding your dreams give you a glimpse of the inner workings of your brain. Psychologists recommend keeping a journal to record what you remember of your dreams upon waking up to help you recognize patterns in your subconscious. It also allows you to exercise your memory!

Please note that this dream guide doesn't imply that your waking hours will be dictated by the interpretations listed here that correspond to your dreams. The human mind is so complex, and the doors in our lives so plentiful that we can choose to make of dreams and life as we wish. It is my hope that you use this as a guide, to help you become aware of your dreams and help you direct your reality.

19477333R00091

Printed in Great Britain
by Amazon